Color and Line

Color and Line

Poems by

Carole Mertz

Cover design by Shay Culligan
Cover art: "Music of the Spheres II"
(2020) by Nancy Boileau (acrylic & cotton string on board)

ISBN: 978-1-952326-80-6

Kelsay Books
502 South 1040 East, A-119
American Fork, Utah, 84003

For my husband, Bob

Acknowledgments

Eclectica: "Dinner with Zukofsky," "The Offspring of a
   Manuscript Defined as Poem"
Mom Egg Review: "Conchalina, My Mystery"
Muddy River Poetry Review: "Lethe's Slim Threads Caught"
Page & Spine: "On Hearing a Mandarin Poem"
Prairie Light Review: "The Changing Colors of Skin"
Pyrokinection: "Conchalina, My Mystery"
Quill & Parchment: "Waiting to Sail"
The Ekphrastic Review: "A Dark and Rainy Night," "Alouette, Au
   Lapin Agile," "As a Father Shows Compassion to His
   Children," "Cornell's World," "Expectant," "Flying Toward the
   Light," "Francois Enjoys an Evening," "Free," "Learned
   Ladies," "Salome," "Secrets," "The Emotion of a Painting,"
   "The Ivy and the Holly," "The Word in Joseph's Hand,"
   "Waiting," "Working the Fields"
The Soc. of Classical Poets: "Greening Fields"
Toward a Peeping Sunrise: "Dinner with Zukofsky," "That this
   Blue Exists," "Waiting to Sail," "Waking"
Voices de la Luna: "Waking"
Wilda Morris Blogspot: "Flow, River, Flow," "That This Blue
   Exists"

Preface

There's a freedom to writing ekphrastic poetry that appeals to me—one can allow the artworks to speak directly and in specifics or one can muse on the artist's intentions and leave unanswered questions.

At times I research the artists and introduce a bit of their history into my writing. Often first impressions work themselves onto my pages and I let them stand. Sometimes I allow myself free rein to stray into open pastures.

Whatever the case, this volume includes ekphrases on canvases created as early as 1555 and as recent as 2019. I've included free verse, prose poems, and shorter forms, as well.

No large 'eggs in cages' here (as per Magritte), only simple descriptions that sometimes wander outside their confines. Julian Barnes, art critic and connoisseur, has declared art doesn't simply capture the excitement of life, but actually becomes that thrilling experience. This is what I experience viewing artworks, whether on the page or on the canvas. I hope to share some of that excitement with you and I hope this book affords you some entertainment.

Contents

A. Colors on the Canvas

Flying toward the Light	15
Alouette, Au Lapin Agile	16
The Changing Colors of Skin	17
The Emotion of a Painting: The Final Test	18
On Hearing a Mandarin Poem	19
As a Father Shows Compassion to His Children	20
white droplets sprinkle	21
A Dark and Rainy Night	22
Smothered	23
billowing leaves cast	24
a flash of bright red	25
Cornell's World	26
Come Share a Glass with Me	27
That This Blue Exists…	29

B. Beton Speaks

Expectant	33
Lethe's Slim Threads Caught	34
uninvited snake	36
The Bequest	37
At Home in Hatboro	38
Conchalina, My Mystery	39
Dinner with Zukofsky	41
Greening Fields	42
Working the Fields	43
O Earth of Winter's Night	45
old rusty key turns	46
Flow, River, Flow	47

C. Syncretia

hummingbird arrives	51
Waking	52
Antediluvian Glimpses	53
Keats Revisited	54
Free	55
Waiting	57
Salome	58
Secrets	59
Learned Ladies	60
Syncretia	61
A Breezy Cinquain	62
Waiting to Sail	63
The Ivy and the Holly	64
The Word in Joseph's Hand	65
The Offspring of the Manuscript Defined as Poem	66
Francois Enjoys an Evening	67

A. Colors on the Canvas

Open wide the mind's caged door,
She'll dart forth, and cloudward soar

—John Keats
fr. *Fancy*

Flying toward the Light

Inspired by *The Best is Yet to Come,* Lorette C. Luzajic (2019)

> *Wake up, O sleeper,*
> *rise from the dead,*
> *and Christ will shine on you.*
> *Ephesians 5:14b*

A near void forms the middle, (you can't quite comprehend the core), but two planes are flying, speeding us to the outer world. This benevolent world, so rich! You love its clutter, not knowing where to place things, happy in the jumbled environment. Your son's presence added to the wondrous mix. It was not an easy A-B-C, you had to make decisions, just as her canvas must have called for decisions. 'Ought-nine' was that split second when decisions were made for you. You feel again the energy of that moment. Look! See again the seconds that are flying away—past the jumbled edifices, past the bursts of energy, past things known, lost, and found again, past constructions that do not fail. Mark the elements that bring you joy! Look for the encouragers! Stretch your arms to the sunlight!

Melded into light
Marked for something stellar bright
Asking what comes next

Alouette, Au Lapin Agile

You liked visiting the famed cabaret,
visited, as well, by Utrillo,

Picasso, and others famed in former
days, their paintings hanging there,

brushed by Yesterday's collected
dust and smell of cooking grease.

What trusting tones from muted talk,
what pretty French chansons! What

press of crowds, squeezed onto
the wooden benches. And somehow

Picasso revisits, and Hemingway's
seated there too—and from songs

at the center you recall events
told in childhood fables. And you

muse on that rabit-ty thief who made off
with many of your best memories.

The Changing Colors of Skin

Though I had no ideographs
like those of a Chinese girl,
I relished the joy of selecting
the colors from the crayon
box. Age, seven years,
my hair was curled by Mother
into fascinating long ringlets,
fascinating even to me.

The marks I made on the page
were likely the first chapters of
my little-girl life. Frustrated though,
I had no just-right color for skin. That
changed, Crayola adjusted. Our
world adapted, too, into these
many new shades of skin. Life
became fascinating, like my curls.

The Emotion of a Painting: The Final Test

After Vawdavitch, Franz Kline (1955)

Is this the text of a bold Japanese printmaker? Or a drawing, perhaps, of a child of four gone magic-marker-wild, luxuriating in the strokes of his unpracticed hand? Marked by a child's reckless glee? (I could show you my son's paintings at four.)

No, this *Vawdavitch* hails from Kline of Wilkes Barre, a place mere miles from my old Pennsylvania homestead. What drew me to his abstract message? It was the awareness of his anger, and perhaps my own; a warning that anger must be treated with care, lest it consume us. In his virile strokes I saw the touch of Pollock, his seeming randomness. I saw the foreboding: the deep-dark, coal blackness against the white, Kline's life robbed of a father, later a mother, and then a wife.

While subways rumbled and smells of fresh rye bread pervaded the room, my friend's Pollock hung in his foyer, at the end of a long kitchen. Haphazard, I'd have said in those days. But now I read more into these abstracts, Kline's included. The premeditated strokes bespeak tumult, the chaotic artistic lives of New York's 1960s, "flower" songs, Viet Nam, feminism, perverse sexual freedoms already erupting, the careless disregard for babies. In this *Vawdavitch,* the anger serves its purpose: the vindication for fatherless Kline, of all that wasn't, but could have been.

On Hearing a Mandarin Poem

They heard him
read his poem
speaking first in English
then his native Mandarin.

Listening straight up close—
Did he render more passion
in English
or in his mother tongue?

No, his intonations were surely
as firm in one as in the other.
Emotion is emotion,
no matter which language read or sung.

As a Father Shows Compassion to His Children

After The Domino Players, Horace Pippin (1943)

Balanced so well, with its whites
and blacks, its reds, the colored richness
of the room's elements, conceals
the poverty endured.

Greatgrandma smokes a pipe, grandma
busies with scissors and thread, mother enjoys
the repartee and clack-clack of the tiles
and the boy—all four, warmed by the stove's
ample heat, an empty coal bucket
standing by and the teapot ready to boil.

The stovepipe carries the heat upstairs
and on the beds, the quilts are spread.
It's 8 o'clock. Soon all four will ascend
the rickety stairs,

a pot of stew left to simmer
for the late-returning worker. He's
done his job; the soup will warm him.
He'll rake the ashes to still the stove,
climb the stairs in the dark and fall into bed.

In '43 Pippin lets us see moon-illumined
clouds on a dark November night. American
troops have landed at Salermo, but Germany
has already begun counterattacks.

white droplets sprinkle
oak leaves in the rainy night—
sending weeping sounds

A Dark and Rainy Night

After Rainy Night at Etaples, William Edouard Scott (1912)

> *He covers the sky with clouds;*
> *he supplies the earth with rain*
> *Ps. 147:8*

An inky-dark place

    pushes down on them

from night's bleak horizon

They seek the limen

    which will welcome them—

Isolated, yet not alone,

    the two trudge

through dark blue corridors

burdened and bleary-eyed,

    weakened but sanguine

Smothered

After Fin de la Jornado, Emilio Boggio (Venezuela, 1912)

The texture of *Fin de la Jornado* is like a heavy tapestry. Overall dark, but with slight elements of gentle pinks, yellows and blues. But these tones are diminished by the more dominant blacks and muddy browns of the foreground. The darkness here is abominable, truly the end of the road. And the way is hard. There is no future and the nearer we come to a point of arrival, the more we see only darkness and lost hope, nothing more. The little house on the river might have carried us away, but it has no fluidity. Seated on water, it nevertheless remains grounded. An unlikely home, it offers no purpose and no respite. The passing women push heavily laden carts, burdens too heavy for their bodies; nothing provides relief. There is no camaraderie on the path—no one greets another. What a cheerless end of a journey! Painted late in his life, Boggio had already said his farewells. One journey remained, a final return to France which had provided him his education and profession. Neither his French-Spanish mother nor his Italian father had fostered any hope to feed his soul. Oh, pauvre Boggio! Your few colors in this painting, those gentle pinks, yellows, and blues plead only a pittance of solace. Your heavy tapestry smothers me.

billowing leaves cast
shadows on window panels
sun shines: shadows flee

a flash of bright red
cardinal in the garden:
Audubon appears

Cornell's World

Each of the stoppered jars,
five and six to a shelf,
shines with directed light
above and mirror behind.

Crystals, beads, seeds,
shells, berries, and bark;
shavings, sand, leaves,
and more draw us into
apothecary folklore.

But this is Cornell's
world, not ours; a place
where he can safely relate
to small and varied things,

placing them in the order
he devises. Are the jars
sealed with O-rings, we
wonder. How pleasing

to see them snugly
encased. How pleasing
to see their tinted
green sheen

Come Share a Glass with Me

On La Guinguette, Vincent Van Gogh (1886)

Van Gogh presents his *La Guinguette* in muted tones. It is a sweetly balanced painting in several ways. Its rosy beiges meet oranges and browns overlaid with touches of greens to represent the trees and what may be ivy above the trellises. This is a quiet scene, but I wonder about the hidden relationships of the ten people present in the scene.

A French dictionary describes the *guinguette* as a small cabaret either with or without a small dance hall where people can gather to drink a cheap "but malicious" light green wine.

Van Gogh painted his Guinguette with four alcoves in the middle distance. These are airily separated, one from the other, by bent-wood trellises. Couples are seated in these alcoves and glasses and bottles are faintly visible. What do the people discuss? Do they talk of the rising price of cabbage? That Jeanne will meet Pierre after his shift ends?

Three rustic wooden tables and benches fill the foreground with one bench situated askance from its table. In the foreground, a bustled woman sits engrossed with her partner. Nearly each of the figures wears a hat, but for the waiter who stands near-center, in a place of importance.

Behind the alcoves is a building to the right whose 32-paned window adds airiness and whose brilliant orange slanted roof points toward a towered structure to the left. Around the tower flies a bird, a very large bird, that seems out of proportion.

Viewers of this painting may enjoy the way the gas lamp in the foreground rises up to meet the corner of the orange roof in the distance. Here is overall balance of composition.

27

I love the quiet tone of friendship as seen in those seated at the tables; most appear relaxed but engaged. The figure who dominates the scene, however, is the waiter standing immobile, patient, nonchalant, but attentive. In his sober black jacket and pants, wearing a very long white apron, he's emblematic of something particular. He seems to speak the sentiment, "As long as this cabaret exists, as long as you, my people, visit, I'll be here to serve you."

We must not pity him, as Orwell in another era, advises us. For *le garçon* stands proudly, as servant, dreaming perhaps of the day when he will sit at leisure like his customers.

I learned the popularity of guinguettes died out when the cheap wine could no longer be had, when Parisians no longer swam in the nearby Seine. Their habits changed; they no longer came to the guinguette for a relaxing glass of that light green wine. In the meanwhile, Van Gogh's scene lives on, permeated with conviviality. Vive l'après-midi!

That This Blue Exists…

I take up a spool of blue thread
determined to thread my way
through the amateur marriage
toward a formidable dinner

at the Homesick Restaurant.
Together we'll be digging to
America; bluets will help us
with our breathing lessons and

the empathy exams
in order to arrive, perhaps,
at Saint Maybe, the place where
she'll chant her usual and

clumsy beginner's goodbye.
We'll continue searching
for Caleb, through the gap
of time, trying to tie together

the sleeper and the spindle.
Together we'll navigate a
patchwork planet, searching
for a distant view of
everything.

B. Beton Speaks

She hurried at his words, beset with fears,
For there were sleeping dragons all around...

John Keats
fr. *The Eve of St. Agnes*

Expectant

After The Staircase, Xavier Mellery (1889)

She ascends the stairs
To clean, perhaps
To offer a bath

But first she knocks
Is the lodger within?

The hallways
Though shadowed

Render order
Stabilized by unknown
Source of light

The shining ceramic
On the stair below
Brings beauty to the scene

The ewer sits expectant
So much of what we hope for
Seems contained therein

Lethe's Slim Threads Caught

I.

Birds flew in across the hearthstone

    out again across the fields

Buds of memory lapped at her feet

    stealing away molested

and unprotected thought

    How to snare and nurture

the fleeting

II.

Heart and hands ached for the recall

    reaching out to no avail

clutching pale slabs of empty air

    "Yours for the taking," winged creatures

taunted and scoffed. Swoosh! she swiped

    at the thieves, murderous in her rancor,

wiped the blood on her sleeve

III.

Where will you go with your unprotected

    mind, with whom share the

minuscules you've known? Certainties, those

    rarities, often rendered as lost,

and beyond recall. Yet that single certainty,

    that singular small thing to which you cling,

will not change. It lingers as sure as a song

uninvited snake
slithers 'neath chrysanthemums
hurry! bring the rake

The Bequest

Virginia Woolf's black snake had
got into my poems,
lurking.

Even in my beaming vanilla ice cream mood,
through all my happiness, I saw
the viper.

I would have struck, or captured it
had it not vanished
in a flash.

Through all my recent successes, nuggets
arrived, offered me on a silver
platter as if individually

wrapped—why the snake? Why now?
Why, just as I stood fortified
and ascending a plane?

Foul one, waiting for my weakest moment, away!
Please send, O God, that precious white
light of truth!

Mary Beton, fallen from her horse, had bequeathed
five hundred per annum. Placed in the coffer,
the gift had made all the difference.

At Home in Hatboro

When they first moved into the town
she heard the train whistle
    daily

She was reading *Nausea,* thought
she was far away in a
    deep valley

She rose up from the valley awakened,
saw it was not a valley
    after all

The library was musty, the train carrying her
to a place of dusty drudgery—
    but still

she was here, in this new town, this nondescript
Hatboro; then the tracks
    disappeared

Sartre promoted his habit of reading
notes found lying on the grass, the pavement, paths leading
    anywhere

Treasures he called them. She began collecting
discards, one scrap after another, a beguiling
    search

But they made no sense; Sartre
had lied to her. Roquentin,
    away with you!

Conchalina, My Mystery

En boca cerrada no entran moscas*

Antoinette of the mountains,
south and west,
sculpted a figurine
I can not comprehend.

Done in brown and white
it's crafted of mud
from the clay of Santa Fe.
And there, on a visit, I bought her.

Little Pueblo figurine,
teach me, through your crafted eyes
and mouth,
the need for silence
or for speech.

She sits there, brown
and clean-white, with legs crossed
and holding a mobile phone.
Looking upward, (mocking perhaps)
her mouth is open,
always open.

Antoinette, the artist, (in the shop)
had explained the injunction
against speaking. Yet here sits
Conchalina, her mouth open
wide. (Someone should admonish her!)

When to be silent, when to speak—
easy to miscalculate.
Conchalina, my little sculpted model,
had I attended more closely,
I might have gained
your mystery.

Flies don't enter a closed mouth

Dinner with Zukofsky

It was 1963. Paul invited his friend Dave
and Dave invited me, his then girlfriend.

The dinner in a Manhattan brownstone
with father and mother, was private;

no others present. Tongue-tied I
merely listened. Knew nothing of his

work and less of Catullus. Didn't know
Celia had written the genders, cases,

and meanings word-for-word
below the Latin lines. Learned

that Catullus was bawdy, but couldn't
discern why Celia had hung such dark

ink-blue and white drapes, so different
from what Mother would have chosen.

Greening Fields

Today I may dream of stubbled fields shriveled
   foretelling of future prospects grim.
If tomorrow's dreams are green, is it a given
   I'll have silos filled to the brim?

Whether fields are bearing or fallow,
   each day's work brings forth its yield,
success evolving securely tomorrow
   by the greater effort today I wield.

In my dream the slopes were shallow
   windswept and covered with a kind of cloth,
surface nutrients protected there,
   shielded against my erring sloth.

I may have gain of whatever kind
   depending on the effort made.
My fields will in their greening shine
   or else lie dormant in the shade.

Working the Fields

After The Angelus, Jean-Francois Millet (1859)

> *He grants peace to your borders*
> *and satisfies you with the finest of wheat*
> *Ps.147:14*

The painter Appleton commissioned it;
the buyer failed to take purchase. Millet
revised his painting—

With the added steeple,
prayers for the potato crop
transform into a sunset prayer,
a rejoicing for Christ's
incarnation. The steeple in
the distance delivers its

meme. More profound,
the prayer of the labor itself
offered by man and woman—
the digging and bending,
the loading and pulling,
the roughening of the palms,
the sweat in the armpits,
the ache in the back—

a plea for health, for strength,
for a generous harvest.

Millet's own devotion is seen
in the laying aside of
the pitchfork, the bent
of the woman's body,

the beneficent sunset across
the fields, the smell of earth,
the light which could be
yet a reverent sunrise
at the ringing of the bells.

O Earth of Winter's Night

Once, we were
appareled in celestial night
when the first day's night had come,

But now,
I can't hear your voice for the wind's cries,
whistling over the bare ground.

Once
the lines…straight and swift between the stars.

But now,
there's fear of the unknown, an uneasiness
gravity will come to an end
like a gray cemetery of felled trees.

The red earth thrums and sighs.
Above the injury—terror, and cold,
not the shadow of cloud and cold,

but waves flowing above the rocks
and birds that came like dirty water.

Winter's dregs made desolate the weakening eye of day;
dusk comes down with its weight of prayer—
all the people on earth had corrupted their ways.

But clingy moon dust visited the earth,
and basalt rock carried by Armstrong.

Keep it, beauty, beauty…from vanishing away.
I grasp that rock, needy with need to grasp
deliverance for Mother Earth.

old rusty key turns,
entrance to ancient building—
opens to new thoughts

Flow, River, Flow

I haven't ridden on swift-flowing rafts,
but I've been swept along in waters
splayed by many a writer's crafts.

I've travelled torrents in books
as varied and bright
as my dream-rich reading nooks.

Petterson (of *Out Stealing Horses*) shows his boy
racing downriver on risky yellow logs,
erupting with violent spurts of joy.

In dread I've watched the swollen Arno strip
gilded paint from Florence's treasures of old.
(K.K. Taylor's diary records this river's slip.)

And what of the Styx? I'd rather not travel
its ominous flows, though Dante and Milton
press me with lines to unravel.

These rivers flow on and on. Never stopping,
I read them again and again,
enjoying vintages of each author's outcroppings.

This River of Words smooths my way,
gift from writers 'round the world.
How wide its reaches I cannot say.

C. Syncretia

Yet even in these days so far retired
From happy pieties, thy lucent fans,
Fluttering among the faint Olympians
I see, and sing, by my own eyes inspired.

John Keats
fr. *Ode to Psyche*

hummingbird arrives
knows its home from prior year—
welcomed like a kin

Waking

There is a stretched space
between the thinking pillow
and tiny tufts of pure thought, though
not knowing, it shrinks from itself, and lies
awhile inert. It turns in its bed of thought
and, touching first light, throws itself
toward a peeping sunrise, vowing: I will
yield. Shrunken now the space
between there and here, between
yesterday and today.

Antediluvian Glimpses

I tell myself I see the ocean
though I haven't touched its shores
since 1987

A brief glimpse of primordial
matter lies embedded in
my hippocampus

or somewhere in the hills
of memory—long ago

and untouched. But resurgences
ring true; yes, there! I see it,

a self-repeating mandala system—
growing, waning, and rebuilding
in antediluvian soils

Keats Revisited

Endymion, beautiful boychild, Zeus's son,
how poets use you e'en today
supporting the immortal lie: Beauteous One,
tending still the slopes of Elis
            'neath swift Selene's ardent ray.

Sleep you still, O Shepherd,
now released from time—
or spend forever restless nights
no longer felt sublime?

Free

After Hors du Cercles, Joan Miro (1920)

You might run in circles, dog-like, but I find
I like your pink background, Miro, it
sends me skyward—I'm rocketed past
those little ink-dots, (stars perhaps?)
while other paths are being

formed—These large black marks are
challenges I need to meet, (the ultimate
right way of seeing things, that's the
challenge). Painted circular blooms are

inventions. (Mother would be proud.) I feel
gentle air on my skin, my limbs are
weightless. Ah, sweet pink, you give me
the space I need—

Those medium-sized inky blobs
are works in progress, perfumed buds ready

to burst. Shall I hitch myself to
existing orbits or lay down new ties?
Surrounded by so much ink, I can't
fail. (Lovely representations!)

Once as a child, I stood before the lilac
tree, squinting into the sun. Daddy
snapped photos, made predictions about
me. I may have surpassed them...I'm out in the pink!

I feel I may go outside the frame. Or I may

dig deeper

       down

               go into the pink behind

that blue bloom on the left.

Oh look! Here's the Morning Star!

Waiting

After Pintura, Joaquin Torres Garcia (1928)

She is not quite refined
She is not quite a trollop
Yet she finds herself in a place she ought
    not to be.

      The café has closed,
      where will she go?

Salome

Flimsily draped
Sassy
All too ready

To follow
Mother's
Greedy footsteps

Messenger
Of God
Soon beheaded

(John neither ate
Nor drank)
His head offered

While Salome
Danced
And danced and danced

Knife in hand
Platter
Dripping holy blood

Secrets

After At the Theatre, Prudence Howard (1928)

Who's to say what secrets
the sisters share, absorbed
in life's shocking melodramas
and still more serious matters.

She looks to her theatre programme
to see if she finds there
answers to dilemmas, desires, and beaus,
and still more serious matters.

But no, it's all about actors
and directors, about mystery—
about love, losses, and discovery,
and still more serious matters.

Many secrets sisters may share; but some
best kept to oneself.

Learned Ladies

After The Chess Game, Sofonisba Anguissola (1555)

The artist positioned young sister well. She stands
"center stage." Her delight, as you can tell, reveals

that big sister holds mama in the clutch. And mama, not
troubled much, looks calmly at her viewer, blithely aware

of nurse standing by. But nurse may have nudged a move
and steered the girl toward her first conquest. Both sisters

know what's about to happen. They stare until the act
is done. Black is positioned, solidly in place. Big sister,

though doubtful, will soon have the king and young
sister can't wait to witness the win.

Syncretia

The word she used was catachrestically
correct (to create a linguistic oxymoron) being
more for untampered logic than against it.

He, however, stammered against her usage
preferring a simpler syntax, one
that could be syncretized in the creation

of new meanings, juxtaposed just
beneath logical lines of comprehension and extending
into quainter thought patterns, positioned

in such a way, all consternation aside, to lead
one into a netherworld unbounded by subject
and verb, very like a liquid logogram, forming a labyrinth

from which, swimming as from the deep and gasping
for breath, one rises into new verbal domains
completely refreshed and ready to begin again.

A Breezy Cinquain

If I
view birds beneath
the tree out front, my mind
soon sees boats sailing aloft a
green breeze

These I
see as freedom
to explore unknown sites,
their histories revealing new
delights

Waiting to Sail

After Luncheon of the Boating Party, Auguste Renoir (1880-81)

Fourteen figures, (a story
with too many characters perhaps?)
gathered quay-side
for the boating trip
to follow the luncheon party.

He painted the wide
amiable scene of men
and women straw-hatted,
beribboned, and tall men
top-hatted, wrapped in an aura

of summer-glazed camaraderie,
at leisure and lingering with wine
a table beneath the orange-
striped canopy. Flirting. Not caring

if the little dog licked
the chin, or the cloth
rumpled. The surprise of it? All
organized for pleasure, all
staged by the master himself.

There's laughter and music
in the air. "Another glass, Gustave?"
We linger, quay-side, waiting
to sail.

The Ivy and the Holly

After "Gogol's Dream," Viktor Gontarov (1995)

He doffs his hat lovingly
with the tip of his heart.
She, half-eaten by the fish,
looks away demurely.

The horses, contented,
await with curiosity. It's
Christmas in the land,
announced by the green—

The wistful scene,
offered in simplicity.

The Word in Joseph's Hand

After Saint Joseph with the Infant Jesus, Guido Reni (1635)

The Word become Incarnate
Is held in Joseph's hand.
He liberates His children,
Brings peace to all the land.

> Give thanks to God our Lord;
> To Him be all the glory
> For e'er remains the Word.

The Word in freshest styling
Who shares all human need.
The Babe and Papa smiling,
The all-embracing Seed.

> Give thanks to God our Lord;
> To Him be all the glory
> For e'er remains the Word.

The Word rebukes all folly,
We live by His command.
With ivy and with holly,
'Tis Christmas in the land.

> Give thanks to God our Lord;
> To Him be all the glory
> For e'er remains the Word.

The Offspring of the Manuscript Defined as Poem

At the completion of the manuscript the footnotes concerned
her; would they extend too far, run into the next page,
become separated from their main material?

Would the hunter stalking the deer, lose sight of the hind
as it springs, running and leaping away? Would the parent
lose its child? The original work its meaning?

Down the long thought-avenues, turning this way and that—
what chance for the runaway? What chain to be linked? What
field enclosed? All, all is a matter of choice. Relinquish

your feral call; return to your pasture. Let the wild remain wild.
At night the signifiers bounced behind the stag's eyes
in the moon's hoary light, lost again as day rose. Rediscovered

in a moment's unspent time, taken hold of, the poem fastened
forever to your welcoming bosom, born of an unsprung,
unseeded process of generation, but fixed, at last, and bounded.

Francois Enjoys an Evening

After White Soup Bowl, Anne Vallayer-Coster (1771)

It's a very heavy cooking pot made of twice-baked clay. Do you
hear the lid scrape the lip of the pot? Do you smell the onion soup
brewing within, ready to receive the muenster?
When you indulge, you must allow the strings of cheese to keep
you tethered to your bowl, and let the conversation float around
you, not distracting you from the onion bouquet, the liquor of the
soup.
For, to be sure, you are surrounded by friends, and the talk is
lively. But they can get on without you; imbibe the rich *fond* and
the cheese, savor your Sauvignon now and again.
And the bread awaits—the bread whose raisins will mix well with
the broth. Ah! How charming that young girl looks, across at the
table to the left. Her father, busy with the chatter, does not see her
drop her napkin and reclaim it, the curls of her rich brown hair
falling briefly across her face, concealing for a moment her wide,
dark, and beautiful child-eyes.
Here is deep satisfaction. To view this beauty, to fill the stomach,
to laugh at the remarks of friends! Suddenly I hear the slow, restful
phrases of Gregorian chants toning from a distance. One needs
nothing more. Only to receive the heat of the broth, to smile and
touch the arms of friends, to give thanks and breathe.
Come now, must you gush so, my friend?
Yes, for the night is perfect and I'll never see another such. Ah,
look! The little girl with the beautiful curls becomes restless.
Father wipes his mustache; after tipping, he bids his companions
goodnight and rises to carry his daughter home.

Notes

The allusion to René Magritte in the Preface refers to Magritte's surreal painting *Elective Affinities* of 1932 in which he depicted a very large egg within the confines of a cage.

P. 16. *Lapin Agile,* the 19th C. cabaret in Montmartre, where artists met, was once called "Where the Thieves Meet." The sign above it, showing a leaping rabbit, was made by Andre Gill. Picasso painted "Au Lapin Agile" in 1905, bringing world fame to the site.

P. 26. Joseph Cornell lived in Flushing, N.Y., near an area where I resided for years. He and his mother cared for his brother who was disabled. Cornell loved collecting sundry objects and displaying them in shadow boxes.

P. 29. "That This Blue Exists…" is a Title Poem. This one uses titles of works by fourteen authors shaped into a little story. It won a 1st Place at a Wilda Morris Poetry Challenge.

P. 45. "O Earth of Winter's Night," a cento poem, borrows lines from Wordsworth, Dickinson, Glueck, Stevens, Smallwood, Sorensen, Genesis 6, and Hopkins.

P. 65. "The Word in Joseph's Hand" is a hymn. It may be sung to the tune "Lo, How a Rose E'er Blooming."

In gratitude

Thanks to Karen Kelsay and the dedicated staff of Kelsay Books for their expertise and courtesy. Special thanks to Nancy Boileau for her beautiful cover art, and thanks to the blurb writers.

Thanks to Marjorie Tesser at Mom Egg Review and to Lorette C. Luzajic at The Ekphrastic Review for showing me the many ways poetry can be created, enjoyed, and shared.

Thanks to Kendra, my special promoter. Thanks to my friends at Calvary L.C. who are such good listeners. And thanks to my readers.

Dearest thanks to Carol who's been a friend and mentor all along, and to my family: to Bob and Ron, to Nan and Wally. Your love means so much.

About the Author

Carole Mertz is a graduate of Oberlin College with a concentration in music performance and fine arts. She is Book Review Editor at Dreamers Creative Writing, a Member of the Prize Nominations Committee at The Ekphrastic Review, and served as advance reader for Women's National Book Association's 2018 poetry contest. Carole judged (in formal verse) the 2020 Poets and Patrons in Illinois International Poetry Contest.

Carole maintains her appreciation of the fine arts following her attendance at The Mozarteum Akademie in Salzburg, Austria. She critiques in fiction, poetry, and essay and has published poems and reviews in literary journals in U.S., Canada, Africa, Great Britain, and India; among them *Arc Poetry, Copperfield Review, CutBank, Into the Void, Main Street Rag, The Bangalore Review, With Painted Word,* and *World Literature Today.* Carole is both a contributor to, and reader for *Mom Egg Review.*

Her writing has also appeared in *Writing After Retirement,* Editors Smallwood and Redman-Waldeyer, Rowman & Littlefield (2014), *Journal VII* of the Society of Classical Poets (2019), and other anthologies. With her husband, she published a series of devotions in *Portals of Prayer,* Concordia Publishing House.

Carole is the author of the poetry chapbook *Toward a Peeping Sunrise,* Prolific Press (2019). She resides with her husband in Parma, Ohio where she is organist and member of Calvary Lutheran Church.

www.ingramcontent.com/pod-product-compliance
Lightning Source LLC
Chambersburg PA
CBHW071357090426
42738CB00012B/3142